Bittersweet Euphoria

The Dating Life of Women of Color

Jasmine Herod

Copyright © 2018 Nuance Publishing

All rights reserved. No part of this book may be reproduced or transmitted in any form or by any means, electronic or mechanical, including photocopying, recording or by any information storage and retrieval system, without written permission from the author, except for the inclusion of brief quotations in a review.

ISBN-13: 978-0692143995
ISBN-10: 0692143998
Printed in the United States of America

Table of Contents

Introduction 5

Preface | LOVE CONNECTION 7

Chapter 1 | FUCKBOYS AREN'T JUST FOR FRIDAY 9
    The Fuckboy Epidemic 9
    Fuckboy Roll Call 10
    That Bullshit - We Can't Make This Up 12

Chapter 2 | THE FUTURE IS FEMALE 17
    #FBF Flashback of Feminism 17
    Who Runs the World? 19
    The "F" Word 20

Chapter 3 | #FORTHECULTURE 23
    Clothed in Strength 23
    Ashes to Side Chicks 24
    Blame Game 25
    Jungle Fever 30
    What You See is What You Get 32

Chapter 4 | GIRLS WHO LIKE GIRLS 37
    This Closet is Cramped 37
    Haters' Gone Hate 39
    #LesbiansBeLike 40

Chapter 5 | KEEP IT 100 41
    It's Not You, it's Me 41
    Our DNA Can't Be Trusted 41
    8 Signs it's a Situationship 42
    The Friend Zone 43
    Recognizing and Understanding Your Power 45

CONCLUSION 49

INTRODUCTION

Being a 90's kid was the BEST! As a kid, I was a Disney movie fanatic. I had to have every Disney movie as soon as it came out on VHS (throwback!). I was begging my mom to buy it for me. I was specifically obsessed with Aladdin (yes, because my name is Jasmine and I wanted to be a princess). Cinderella and Snow White were also in heavy rotation. I was a sucker for the perfect love story at an early age. As a child all you see is a pretty princess, great songs, a handsome prince, and a happily ever after love story. My perception of love and the journey to finding it was misconstrued by every Disney movie. Love at first sight happens all the time, a man will complete your life, being a damsel in distress will get you your prince, and finding love is easy, were just a few ideals that were consistent in Disney movies. Now, I am a 29 year old, single Black woman and have realized that the love stories I grew up watching are nowhere close to my reality. Actually, they are complete lies! Love is a battlefield. Jordan Sparks was spot on! Finding love is hard, finding love as women of color can be harder. Why? Our experiences in this world are different: in college, at work, hanging out with our friends, at restaurants, dealing with law enforcement, civil rights, and discrimination. Dating is no different. Our experiences in many, if not every facet of life, is different from White women's, those are the facts. That is why this book is for us! There isn't one like it. What we have to endure while dating, hell, while living, is not just because we are women. It is racially and culturally charged which brings in an element that White women do not have to encounter. Have you ever read a book that was just for women of color? Discussing what we encounter within a safe space for us to be open and honest about the frustrations of being single millennial women of color? Now you have one. I want every woman who reads this book to feel a connection to another sister of color. Regardless of cultural or ethnic background, we are all fighting the same fight; we are all connected to each other. You are not going through these treacherous single waters alone; many are having the same difficulties and have some of the same crazy stories. Many of us have all dated online, or know someone who has, had a fuckboy or two (or three), have been deemed 'undateable' due to our culture or skin color, have been the victim of stereotyping, have hidden who we really are, entered into relationships we knew weren't a good idea, etc. We have all been there. What's crucial is that we learn from these situations and become better women by learning from each other. Ultimately, I want every woman to look at this book as a journey to a better understanding of self and her sisters. Growth is inevitable, uncomfortable, and necessary to make it through life; and by the end of this book, I hope we all have grown into stronger, more understanding women.

PREFACE

LOVE CONNECTION

You can't listen to Pandora, watch television, or get on social media without seeing an ad for an online dating website promising you that the love of your life has logged on and is waiting to meet you. The free trials and the actors they use on the ads start to make you curious, "Is my husband on Match?" Or, "Maybe I should try Tinder and Black People Meet." When you finally get past the thoughts of "Am I really that desperate to try online dating?" you sign up. For the first few days, maybe even weeks, you look forward to logging in and seeing all the eligible singles in your area that you probably would never run into on the street. It's like shopping online for men and you are hooked! You check your profile more than your texts, emails, and Facebook combined. You begin to get messages from men telling you how beautiful you are and how they would love to meet up for a cup of coffee or brunch on Sunday; you're geeked, finally meeting men on your level. As you talk to these men, their messages are very sexual and borderline disrespectful. "I've never dated a Black woman, I need some chocolate, and I heard you all are the best!" As if being with a Black woman was on his bucket list. "Wow! Your pictures look very classy and you're well educated, I like that." Thinking that this is typical of non-Black men, you let it go. You then match with a very handsome Black man. As the conversation begins to get deeper, he says "I'm surprised by how you carry yourself. You're very well spoken. These other Black chicks are loud and always ready for some drama." You tell yourself to just ignore it and move on; there are plenty other men in your inbox anyway. Well those men, Black or non-Black, mimic the sentiments of the first two conversations. Eventually, you stop checking your messages and jump at the mere vibration of your phone letting you know you had a new match or message. Dating online for a woman of color is not always an enjoyable experience. We are denied the fun and charm of asking about occupation, and favorite restaurants. Many of us feel like we must first uncover the belief system of men we barely know to see if their beliefs match ours. Am I just a conquest? Do you understand the politics around my ethnicity or religion? What are your thoughts on Black Lives Matter? Are you a Trump supporter? Dating for women of color is a constant reminder that you are not your own person, you are every Black, Arabic, Latino, African woman this man has every come in contact with including the women he sees on television and movies. He takes those judgements and stereotypes, and judges you against women he has never met.

Not every story ends like mine. Many women that have tried online dating are very successful. I attended a wedding of a close friend who married a wonderful man that she met on Tinder two years prior. One night while bored, she decided to get on Tinder just for fun. She came across a guy she thought was attractive and swiped right, they eventually matched. No other thought was given on her part until he slid in her DM's a few days later. Their first date was instant chemistry and they have been inseparable ever since and were married in 2017 and are so in love!

> He first came in my inbox to introduce himself and state his intentions; I thought 'this guy has to be a joke'. I was honestly not trying to buy it. I am so happy I didn't get in my own way.
>
> *~Latin American Woman*

Dating is difficult and in many ways online dating makes it easier. Just be aware of the pitfalls that you may encounter as a woman of color. The ignorance is real, ladies, but it doesn't mean you have to deal with it. Keep it pushing, try another dating site, change your preferences, or just meet people the old-fashioned way. It worked for the last few decades and I don't think it will ever become obsolete. It is about the journey and online dating may be a part of yours. Embrace it and enjoy the experience. You may find Mr. Right, if you don't find Mr. Right, at least you will have some great stories to tell your girls. Happy hunting!

PERSONAL CHALLENGE

Do you want to give online dating a try? DO IT! Just because it didn't work for me and some other women doesn't mean it will not work for you! Take a leap of faith, try something new, and no I don't mean Tinder, if you're going to do something, do it right. Go with sites like Match.com or EHarmony.

CHAPTER 1

FUCKBOYS AREN'T JUST FOR FRIDAY

The Fuckboy Epidemic

If dating was a board game, the ultimate rule to win the game would be to avoid fuckboys at any cost! Unfortunately, they know the short cuts to winning the game; and making women look dumb is their favorite move. As women, many go through a fuck-girl stage. But as we mature, we understand that our fuck-girl decisions have fuck-girl consequences and eventually we get tired of living that way and reform. However, I assume most men never get the memo that the way they are treating women will eventually come back on them ten-fold. It seems like the number of fuckboys have quadrupled over the last few years, leaving women asking, "WHERE ARE THE GOOD MEN?" I have had my fair share of fuckboys and so have many of the women who are featured in this book. Fuckboys are more common than Trump tweets; and just as annoying! So, you may be asking yourself, "What is a fuckboy?" If you have to ask, congratulations you've never dated one. Keep up the good work! A fuckboy is a guy that uses a combination of charm, lies, deception, and his good looks to get the attention of women to do nothing but waste her time. They are the type of men who ask you out on a date and stand you up, the kind that text you exclusively after 10 P.M., tell you they aren't ready for a relationship, but want all the perks, send "Hey stranger" text messages, always want you to come over to "chill," and constantly ask you for sexy pics. In a nutshell, they are the worst and need to be avoided at all cost. Not just to save you the time and effort, but to save you the mental stress that their presence brings. Where did the fuckboy come from? Many theories have been presented over the last few years. Many believe that all fuckboys come from their upbringing, being around men that have treated a woman poorly is passed down to the next generation. Some believe they are made by women, and if we just didn't accept their fuckboy ways there wouldn't be any to begin with. Well, regardless of where they come from we still have to deal with them, so we might as well be smart about it.

Fuckboy Roll Call

Going through life and not running into at least one fuckboy is hard, so education is key! There are many different categories of fuckboys. I have compiled a list of the most common so you can spot one before they make their move or at least before you fall for one.

The *"We Don't Need A Label"* Fuckboy
He will give you every reason that a label means nothing and the connection is more important, he will treat you like you are his one and only; you aren't.

The *"Out-N-Proud"* Fuckboy
He just doesn't care, he's living his fuckboy life to the fullest with no regrets. This is the easiest fuckboy to spot; he embodies many of the classic fuckboy attributes. He will not be "ready" for a relationship, he will not take you out, you are not the only woman in his life, he lies, and you're always "crazy" or "being too sensitive" when you question his actions.

The *"Reappearing"* Fuckboy
- He does a great disappearing and reappearing act. Everything is going well; he is nice, taking you on dates, etc. Hell, he even met some of your friends. All of a sudden he disappears to never be heard from again. Months go by, you get a "hey stranger" text from an unsaved number (of course you deleted his contact, who wouldn't?) Yup, it's the reappearing fuckboy. He sensed you had moved on and wanted to mess with your head some more, because this fuckboy is the ultimate opportunist. Don't reply, move on!

The *"Nice Guy"* Fuckboy
This one is the toughest to spot. The best example for this type of fuckboy is Lawrence, from the HBO show Insecure. Lawrence is the super nice guy that fell down on his luck, lost his job, and his girl, Issa. In his effort to move on, he begins to date a woman, Tasha. After dating Lawrence for a while, she invites him to a family gathering. Of course being a good guy Lawrence attends, but leaves for a work event, and never returns to Tasha's family event; leaving her alone, confused, and most importantly, embarrassed. Tasha, who is rightfully upset, says "You're worse than a fuckboy; you're a fuckboy who thinks he's a good dude." This is the hardest fuckboy to spot, and in some situations the hardest one to understand. I truly believe they have good intentions, but somewhere in his decision making the fuckboy in his system takes over and the guy you came to like is nowhere to be found.

The *"Emotionally Unavailable"* Fuckboy
He has the communication skills of a two year old. Actually, they communicate better than this guy! When you share your feelings with him, he will probably disregard them and not share his own. Not out of cruelty, he just has no idea how to process your feelings and share his own. He doesn't know how to put his feelings into words so he keeps everything bottled up, trying to get him to open up to you will exhaust you mentally. Don't waste your time, sis, it is not worth it!

The *"Clueless"* Fuckboy
This guy doesn't even know he is a fuckboy, or he is just playing dumb. Either way, he is a handful. When you try to explain his fuckboy actions to him, he is clueless as to why you are so mad at him. He will never change until he sees a problem with his actions, bye!

The *"Sexist"* Fuckboy
This guy is the worst. Ladies, he is the guy that will tell you why a woman should uplift her man more than she uplifts herself, "My light should shine brighter than yours and you should help me with that" or, "You should be my biggest cheerleader," he says. He may also quote bible verses to explain to you why women should be completely subservient to their husband and the only way is to forsake their happiness. Is there some truth to this? It depends on who you ask. In my opinion, WE are each other's biggest cheerleaders. This is a team effort, and there is no 'I' in team. He is also anti-feminist and will tell you why feminism has ruined women and our society as a whole.

The *"Entitled"* Fuckboy
The man who thinks you should have sex with him because he is, well, him. He thinks he is God's gift to women and he spreads his gift to anyone and everyone. NEXT!

The *"Mindfuck"* Fuckboy
He is also known as the smooth talker or manipulator. Watch out for this one. He will have you apologizing to him when you have caught him with another woman.

Unfortunately, there are too many fuckboys in this world to cover them all, but ladies, we have women's intuition for a reason. If he seems suspect, he probably is. Go with your gut!

PERSONAL CHALLENGE

If it looks like a duck and quacks like a duck, it's a damn duck! Take a close look at the man or men in your life. Do they fit into any of the categories? Are their intentions with you questionable? Are you getting played? Don't be afraid to address your concerns with your guy. His response may be all you need to answer these important questions.

That Bullshit- We Can't Make this Up

My male friends tell me that the dating stories I share with them cannot be true, men aren't that bad, and women are over exaggerating to make men seem worse than they really are, because we love to male bash. Well, it's time to prove them wrong. Ladies, we are imaginative and very creative, but this bullshit, we cannot make this stuff up if we tried and I'm sure we wouldn't want to.

> I've known this guy my entire life. He's 38, no kids, nice life, God fearing, and not to mention a Kappa. He made the first move and reached out to me as a business consultant. We started off as friends discussing ways of starting a youth program in our home town seeing as I work in the same field. Well, after that we went on a few dates and he was a complete gentleman. Opened doors, forehead kisses, expressive dates, back and body massages with no sex at this point even discussed. He met my son for the first time and it was an instant connection, which is very important to me because my son's father signed his rights over to me at the age of two. He never judged me or made me feel anything but happiness. After three months of dating, we had sex. Afterwards, we went to sleep and he held me all night. I woke up to breakfast in bed, laughs and more sex. After that the calls slowed down, the texts became shorter, the dates stopped and he went from liking me so much to wanting to focus more on God and his career. Now what's strange is I've asked him if we were okay and of course he said 'Yes.' He stopped trying so I basically gave up, but what guys don't understand is those things literally break a woman down. Now he feels he's not ready to jump in a relationship. Why couldn't you have said that three months and five fucks ago! We are now just friends and I'm not sure where it's going at this point.

~Black Woman

My very first love! Hell, first everything was a complete fuckboy! His name was Greg and we met when I was 14! He was on a "pass" from the juvenile detention center, which should have been my first red flag! He was a bad boy, middle school dropout, rude as fuck to his mama and an all-around menace to society, but still I fell hard! He called one night and told me (not ask me) he was coming to get my 15 year old ass. How? With no license? But still I didn't give a fuck, I was game! I snuck out of the house and went to a friend's house where he then tried to have sex with me and I wouldn't so he put me out! Yes! In the middle of nowhere! I had to be at least 20 minutes away from home! So I started walking, then running, then crying. I eventually called my mom, she picked me up and drove me back to my dad's and coached me on how to sneak back in and I did exactly as I was told! I didn't offer any explanations! I got back in the house and vowed I would never speak to him again! Ha! Not even two months later I gave that piece of shit my virginity. He became mentally and physically abusive. He was like a cancer, but I continued to be with him. And then one day, I found out I was 16 and pregnant! I was terrified! I told him and he said the typical line,"It isn't mine!" I was furious because I knew he was the only boy I had ever been with. I couldn't figure out why he tested me the way he did! It wasn't love! I told my mom about the pregnancy and that resulted in an abortion! The worst and best thing I could have ever done! Greg brainwashed me into thinking something was wrong with me! He made me think I was not and could not ever be enough for a man! Ultimately, he scarred me! Although I was a teen when I went through that nightmare, I will never forget! Now I'm a mother and my guards are already up for any fuckboy that tries to enter my daughter's life. Not over here, sir! I never want her to endure all the pain I went through, ever! I'm 27 and happily married now, but some of those unhealthy relationship characteristics I learned from Greg has spilled over into my marriage! Regardless of how long ago it was, the anger, pain, fear, trust issues, and insecurities were all issues I had with my husband! I had to learn to let all that resentment go and just fucking move on! And as for that fuckboy Greg, God handled him! He was sentenced to 30 years in jail! For murder!

~*Black Woman*

" I met a guy through mutual friends, and they all thought we would hit it off. We went out on a couple dates and one night went to go see the stars, literally. And that was the night we had sex for the first time. Shortly after that I moved in with him. I cooked for him, cleaned, bought groceries, etc. Everything was going great until one night I was texting him to come over and he didn't reply. Come to find out he was with another girl that night. I let it go and kept dating him. I even met his army buddies, spent NYE with him, and met his brother. He left to go to Alabama for flight training and we still kept in contact. I went to visit him once and found out he had been sleeping with other women there. He came back to visit a couple of times and then when he moved back later that year, I thought we would pick up where we left off and see what happens. Nope! Apparently a girl from Nashville was visiting him and talking to him more than I was and so he slept with both of us. Tried to win him back, stupid me, and still got hurt in the process. When I thought we were over and I was starting the process of getting over him, I found out that I was pregnant with his child. The other woman he was seeing was also pregnant . He had two women pregnant at the same time, I couldn't tell my friends nor could I keep the baby; he however told her to keep her baby. I didn't want to keep the baby, I knew I wasn't ready, I thought it was love and that is supposed to conquer all, right? Yea, I was wrong. It is now two years later, and the experience still angers me, I am slowly moving on. "

~Black Woman

After so many heartbreaks, I thought he was it. I was done looking I had found him and I was ready to settle down and move to Alabama. I had just begun my current career in 2014 as a pharmaceutical sales woman and was in Vegas for job training. I met Gradlin while doing job training in Vegas, and we hit it off right away; staying up late talking about our new jobs and our lives back at home. He showed me pictures of his son, and told me he was ready to settle down and get married. As the week came to an end, we exchanged numbers and talked daily for close to a year. We would see each other at sales meetings each year. We would talk, have fun, and eventually became intimate with each other. After we became intimate our relationship got even better, I was officially falling for him! I even traveled to Atlanta to visit him. He took me everywhere, bought me whatever I wanted, including a pair of Louboutins, and by the time I left our bond was unbreakable. Did I mention he was Black, fine, and educated? I was in heaven and he wanted me! The turning point was when I got a new job and moved to Atlanta for six months. I was so excited to be close to him for such a long period of time. I made the eight hour drive to Atlanta. Halfway there he tells me that he can't help me move in with no explanation. So, me, my mom, and my roommate's boyfriend moved me into my temporary home. I lived in Atlanta for six months and never saw him once. He would make plans, I would change my schedule, and he would stand me up. He would never call and explain. After I left Atlanta, I was done with him. Never answered his calls or texts. Seeing that I was ignoring him, he threatened me for six months that he would post my sexy pictures (yes, he is that type of fuckboy) on Facebook to, "expose me as a hoe." I never responded. Every year on New Year's Day, including New Year's 2018. He will text me and say, "Let's start fresh...It's a new year and I want to make things right, right my wrongs, I don't want to block my blessings" EVERY. SINGLE. YEAR. I never respond.

~Black Woman

PERSONAL CHALLENGE

We all have stories similar to the women featured. If you have a story, share it with your family or close friends. Use your experiences and wisdom to help your fellow sister to not fall in the trap of the fuckboy, caring is sharing!

CHAPTER 2

THE FUTURE IS FEMALE

#FBF Flashback of Feminism

The first wave of feminism had a politically ran agenda. The leader of the Suffrage Movement believed that to first gain the rights they deserved, they must get the right to vote. This wave of the movement is etched in American history. This was the beginning of our fight for equal rights. Elizabeth Cady Stanton and Susan B. Anthony are known in history as the forerunners of the women rights movement. They believed that women were equal to men and could not only own land, but they should be allowed to work, and should have the right to vote since the men in office made decisions for all citizens. Because of their relentless efforts, the right to vote was given to White women through the 19th Amendment. Unfortunately, Black women, who were the majority of the minority at the time, did not receive the right to vote. At the beginning of the women rights movement, Black women including Sojourner Truth, Ida B. Wells and Anna Julia Cooper made it evident that women's voting rights are also Black women's voting rights. The efforts of Ida B. Wells, Anna Julia Cooper, along with other Black women during this time was rejected by the national women's movement. Through this, the Black feminist movement was established by Margaret Murray Washington, the wife of Booker T. Washington, along with Ida B. Wells and many more Black pioneers. They formed the National Federation of Afro-American Women. This later became the National Association of Colored Women. Black Feminism began due to a lack of representation and tolerance of Black women in the national feminist movement. The national feminist movement excluded Black women due to the racism that ran rampant at that time. They believed that if Black women were included, they would not be able to reach their goal of achieving the right to vote, so Black women were left out for the "greater good." Black feminists at this time included Frances Ellen Hawkins, Ida B. Wells and many more that have become forgotten history. The ideals established by these pioneers are still held in high regards today. Sexism, class, and race are all directly linked, but should be considered as separate entities that need their own discussions to completely understand the struggle of the Black woman. These women were fighters during a time where it was dangerous to speak your mind as a woman, especially a Black woman. They could have paid with their lives. Yet, they persisted; and the ideals established became the foundation of the Black feminist movement.

The feminist movement excelled during the 1960's due to the protest of the Vietnam War and the Civil Rights Movement. This was a crucial time for Black feminism. It was evident that the White feminist movement was not interested in inclusion. To make sure their message was heard, their ideals evolved and many more pioneers of the movement began to arise, making it known throughout the civil rights and feminist movement that Black women suffered from racism as well as sexism. Seeing that the civil rights movement was male driven by Martin Luther King, Malcolm X, etc., Black women felt as if their voices were once again not being heard or considered valid.

The Black feminist movement ideals were sharpened during this time by women like Alice Walker who coined the term "Womanist," which is defined as a Black feminist or feminist of color, someone who is committed to the wholeness and well-being of all of humanity, male and female. Womanism identifies and critically analyzes sexism, anti-Black racism, and their intersection. Womanism recognizes the beauty and strength of embodied Black womanhood, and seeks connections and solidarity with Black men.

The Black feminist movement was no doubt a political movement, a fight against not only sexism in an effort to gain the same equal rights White women were fighting for, but also racial, class, and patriarchal oppression. Why? Because all of these separate oppressive entities can and will simultaneously impact all women of color. The second wave of the White feminist movement had excelled into a national movement demanding jobs outside of the home for women, equal pay, and reproductive rights including contraception and pro-choice options. As the two movements evolved simultaneously, they took two different avenues. Black feminism addressed reproductive rights, health care, equal pay for women, access to abortions, violence against women, rape, sexual harassment, police brutality, lesbian and gay rights, and so many more. As the movement grew, so did the organization's affiliations. In the 1970's and early 1980's, thirteen organizations were founded that included all women of color from different class and educational backgrounds working for the greater good of addressing the sexism and racism they all faced regardless of socioeconomic status. Alice Walker, Angela Davis, Barbara and Beverly Smith, and Cheryl Clarke, the founders of the Combahee River Collective, a lesbian feminist group that was greatly influenced by the NBFO (National Black Feminist Organization) and the BWAO (Black Women Organized for Action) was, and still is, viewed as an organization committed to the liberation of women of color from the oppressive culture endured in America. I would advise all women of color that identify as a feminist to read their statements on Black feminism.

Where are we currently in the fight for women's rights? We have definitely come a long way, but we all still have a lot of work to do. Women in America still make less than a man for doing the same job. Asian women- 84.5%, White women-75.3%, Black women- 63.3% Latino women-54.4% of a White male's earnings based on data for median annual earnings for 2015 and 2016. Reproductive rights have improved; companies like Planned Parenthood give women the freedom and control to make their own decisions pertaining to contraception, abortion, and birth options. But this win has been an uphill battle due to lawmakers trying to put restraints on the laws that give women the control to make her own decisions. Do we still have work to do? Of course. Presently, feminism is changing; becoming a force to be reckoned with and not pushed aside easily. Many say we are in wave four of feminism. Which I define with the phrase, "Rumble, young woman, rumble."

For example, the #MeToo and #TimesUp movements are a perfect example of how the fourth wave of feminism is using social media outlets as a platform to spread awareness that violence, sexual harassment, misconduct, sexism, and misogyny against women will no longer be tolerated. We are marching, protesting, and speaking our truth regardless of race, color, or sexual orientation. Is there still a divide between White, Black, and women of color feminism? What can be stated is that the issues that were discussed in the 60's, 70's, and 80's from the leaders of the White and Black feminist movement are still being discussed to this day. With the current standing of America pertaining to police brutality against men and women of color, building the wall, travel bans, the state of our government, mass shootings, gun control, violence against the gay community, violence against women, etc., women of color will always have a different and necessary fight.

PERSONAL CHALLENGE

Are you a feminist? Do you even know what it means to be a feminist? We are surrounded by a society that will jump on any bandwagon because it sounds good or is trending on Twitter. To truly get behind a cause or movement you must understand it to know where your beliefs fit in- if they even do. It is so easy to watch a video or read an article and adopt that person's point of view without forming your own. Feminism has grown so much since the days of Sojourner Truth and Angela Davis, it has taken on a life of its own. Being a feminist can mean something different to every woman that reads this book and that is okay. Feminism at its core is the right for a woman to choose, so choose what kind of woman you want to be and what you want to believe in. So many women before you made sacrifices for you to have that freedom, USE IT!

Who Runs the World?

Girls! We will always run the world, contrary to popular beliefs. We grow human beings inside our bodies, birth them, and then make them functioning members of society. We are the foundation of this world, always have been, always will be. With all that responsibility we are also taking on the corporate world as entrepreneurs, leaders in the government, media, medicine, and fashion. WE ARE TAKING OVER at alarming rates. Our takeover starts on the college level. According to the National Center for Education Statistics, Black women are the highest receivers of bachelor's degrees at 64%, Latino women at 60%, Native American women at 61% and Arabic American women at 60%. We are thriving as entrepreneurs and becoming key players in this profession, we like being our own bosses and making our own rules and are very successful in it. Latino women are the fastest growing business owners, showing a growth of 58% since 2002 bringing in 55.7 billion dollars of revenue. They are out here winning! Women of color are highly represented in the areas of service occupations, especially in the fields of nursing, social work, management, criminal justice, education, etc. However, we are underrepresented in science, engineering, and legal occupations which are dominated by White women, for now! Millennial women are expanding their horizons on what they believe they are capable of achieving, entering fields not only dominated by White women but also by White men. We have a long way to go to dominate certain professional fields, but we are well on our way. No longer are we limiting ourselves or letting others limit us, telling us what profession is a "man's world," or there are not women of color in a particular field. We are entering into fields that were once seen as out of our reach, professions that were closed off to us for decades and the best part is that we are succeeding in them. But with great strides, comes setbacks in other parts of life. With the advances that women have made in education and profession, the advancements are not seen to all as progressive. To some men in our society our advancements are seen as their downfall.

The "F" Word

You hear often, or have even said yourself, that good, available men are hard to find. In our cultures, there are factors working against us when we are trying to find a man to date. I have found that being a feminist is another hurdle that is difficult to get around when dating as well. When sitting across the table from an independent, self-sufficient feminist woman who speaks her mind, in a respectful way, some are turned off by her "masculinity." Her strong opinions about her culture and the use of the "F" word would bring the date to a screeching halt. Let's be honest, men have been benefiting from the oppression of women for decades in one way or another and many are not even aware of their male privilege to address it. So why would they ever want it to stop? While dating, I would find that the men I was dating were okay with me having opinions about everything until we discussed women rights. All of a sudden, I was not "feminine enough." They didn't understand why I was complaining or why I hated men so much. What some do not understand is that feminist movement and ideology is and never has been about making men feel unappreciated or not needed. In a different time, the generations of women before us needed financial security, the only way to get it was by getting married and having a man take care of you financially, which was a form of oppression in and of itself. Times have changed. Women (women of color to be exact) are the most educated groups in America. Which means women marrying for financial security is a thing of the past. We are getting married later in life, building our own wealth, and being a lot more independent. Because of this, men may think they are not needed as much by women because we are making our own money and the role of the "bread winner" has been taken from them. This couldn't be farther from the truth. If a man believes that his sole purpose in a relationship with a woman is to provide financial security, he does not understand all of the dynamics of a lasting, long term relationship, or understand the value that a man can bring to a woman in so many other ways. A woman being a feminist is empowering, but it does not take the place of being loved and giving love in return. Feminism is not anti-man. Dating as a feminist may leave you ready to give up on love all together and finding a significant other who respects and accepts your feminist views and also endorses them himself feels impossible. But now is not the time to abandon your efforts. Never give up! Feminist men do exist and have grown in numbers in previous years; your efforts will not be in vain.

Intelligent women know their worth more than anyone. Unfortunately, it may be harder to find a man that matches and recognizes her worth and intelligence."

~Latin American Woman

I believe men are intimidated by successful women. Successful women tend to be dominant women. Most men feel their masculinity being threatened.

~Latin American Woman

Feminist women just need a man to take control.

~Black Man

PERSONAL CHALLENGE

Do you ever minimize your opinions to appease a man you are dating? You don't want to lose another one, I get it! Is he worth your integrity? Is the possibility of a relationship, just to say you have someone worth silencing yourself? Society already does a pretty good job of doing that for you, do not do it to yourself. Speak your mind and be open to others' opinions, but never silence yourself!

CHAPTER 3

#FORTHECULTURE

Clothed in Strength

In many cultures, dating outside of your race is of the norm. In the Arabic culture, this is not the norm. Their religion and culture are extremely important. The preservation of their unique traditions, language, and customs are so important that dating outside of their race is not acceptable. "What religion will the children be?" "What traditions will they follow?" In the Arabic culture, being true to who you are and true to the ancestors that came before you is important. Important enough that they stay within their race when seeking a mate. With these traditions going back centuries, the millennial Arabic American women face new challenges being American and Arabic, practicing their Muslim religion, upholding centuries of tradition, and adopting the traditional American dating practices. Many men in the Arabic culture still practice and believe in the traditional roles of women in the Arabic culture such as expecting them to cover their bodies, wear hijabs as a sign of modesty, not work, take care of the children to ensure the Arabic religion and traditions are passed down, husbands being head of the household, etc. In other words, men like their control and want to keep it for as long as they can. The millennial Arabic-American women are changing the status quo and making their own rules. The millennial Arabic women are doctors, nurses, nurse practitioners, lawyers, students, mothers, and wives; learning from and breaking through the limited roles of the Arabic women that came before them. They are the first generation of the liberated woman and they are not looking back. No longer accepting the arranged marriages their mothers and grandmothers did has opened them up to choosing for themselves, but with this comes challenges. Women are openly scrutinized for their actions. Arabic women must carry themselves in a certain way; they must talk and dress in a certain way to be more accepted in their culture. When dating, Arabic women run into men that want a traditional Arabic woman; women that stay at home with the children and are more subservient so that the men can have more control. For the Millennial Arabic women this is not acceptable and makes the dating pool shallow. These women are pushing forward, learning from the women before them, evolving their individuality while staying committed to their Muslim faith and Arabic traditions. I call these women my friends, they are amazing!

> **PERSONAL CHALLENGE**
>
> Religion and the traditions that come with it are important in every culture regardless of race, it is our moral compass, what we used to make decisions daily, who we look to for guidance, and who we thank for our blessings. But how much does religion matter in your choice of a mate? Would you date someone outside of your chosen religion? It is more customary in the Arabic community to date and marry someone within your culture for cultural preservation reasons. Is it just as important in the Black or Latino community? Could two people of different religious backgrounds date, marry, and raise children?

Ashes to Side Chicks

The days of fidelity are long gone, or so it seems. Side Chicks are the new fad and everyone has to have one, or two, or maybe even three. Why is this acceptable? I cannot scroll through Facebook without seeing a meme, video, or status about a man having a main chick and a side chick. I am confused. I thought relationships were for two people, not three (unless agreed upon). What really baffles my mind is women are putting up with their man being intimate with another woman. Why? Why is this becoming the norm? I get it, according to women there is a shortage of men due to incarceration, death, sexual preference, the fuckboy epidemic, and many more factors that contribute to there being more single women than there are men. So sharing men is what we have been forced to do? No, I don't believe it. Just like there is a guy code, bros before hoes, even though disrespectful, it has a strong message. Men stick together no matter what; they will even go as far as lying for their homeboy so he can continue his dirt. I'm not saying go that far, but what I am saying is to show some loyalty and respect to yourself first and secondly to your fellow women. When made aware of the situation, choose yourself over a man who will continue to have a chick on the side.

For the women who are the side chicks, are you happy with who you see in the mirror, knowing that you are taking part in hurting another woman? Is he really worth being second fiddle? I am sure he isn't if he thinks that cheating on his main chick is okay. You get some sex and he may take you out to eat, but mostly you're his jump off! It is demeaning and you are worth more than that. If no one has ever told you that or you don't feel like you are, you do not know or understand your power as a woman and you need to take part in an extensive self-exploration. You receive what you allow, put yourself in her shoes, how would you feel if that were you?

For the women that know her man has a side chick and says nothing, I've been there. Having some of him was so much better than not having him at all. You turned a blind eye to his actions, made excuses for him because at times love can be blinding. Everyone around you knew what was happening but knew that telling you was a waste of time. Sis, be brave. Come to terms with the hurt he has caused and the hurt his absence will bring. Cry, throw things, pray, scream, watch Waiting to Exhale as many times as you need.

One day, you will wake up with a light heart and a clear mind and have the ability to move on and eventually open yourself up to being loved by the right man at the right time. That's how it works. Going through heartbreak is sometimes a necessity. The best teacher in life is failure, whether it is at a job, a friendship, or a relationship. It teaches you how to depend on yourself, recognize fake relationships, makes you cautious, and allows you to become a critical thinker who analyzes (but doesn't over analyze) situations before entering them. Think of those traits as war wounds making you stronger and smarter for the next time.

PERSONAL CHALLENGE

Mental health is taken for granted in our society. Many think that if you cannot see the problem then it is not there. We as women do not make our mental health a priority, we put others needs and happiness before our own. We are mothers, daughters, and wives. We have people that depend on us! But we cannot neglect ourselves and expect to take care of our children, man, and important business. **MAKE YOUR MENTAL HEALTH A PRIORITY!** If you are not happy, figure out how to get happy; quit the job (secure another one first), leave that relationship, cut that friend off, take a few hours for yourself (go to the spa, gym, or out with the girls), go to church, whatever you have to do to improve your mental health, DO IT!

Blame Game

Are Black women to blame for Black men choosing to date outside of their race?

I came across a video while researching for this book. It was a clip called "Iyanla Fix My Life: House of Healing the Myth of the Angry Black Woman." In this clip, Iyanla sits down with three Black men as they explain why they do not date Black women. Their reasoning was based on past dating experiences, upbringing, and Black women being too masculine and not knowing their "place." To be honest, as a Black woman, this video was infuriating! I began to get so upset that I wanted to just stop the video and not hear anything else these men had to say. Their reasons were extremely superficial and based off nothing but poor judgement and prejudice. Instead of stopping the video, I kept listening due to curiosity. My suspensions were correct; they had bought into the stereotypes of Black women and decided the best thing for them to do was to avoid them completely. After watching the video, I wanted to dig a little deeper into the notion that Black women are to blame for their singleness. I reached out the community and got mixed reviews from the question above. It was an interesting interaction and I definitely started some heated debates.

Black men are constantly putting down and disrespecting Black women, and for some reason are the biggest critics of Black women and everything they do. Don't get me wrong, some people have a preference, but usually it is backed with shallow, non-fact based internal issues that they have and need to deal with.

~Black Man

Being a nerdy Black guy back in the day was never well received. I was told I talked "white" and I didn't quite fit in. I was looking at who the Black girls were choosing and I was nothing like them. I was just a comic book reading, video game playing, non-athletic Black dude. Black girls were not feeling me like that so I dated outside my race. I never hit a point where I was not into Black women, I just understood how things worked, and they weren't into me so I had no choice but to look elsewhere.

~Black Man

I absolutely cannot stand a Black man who dates outside of his race because he believes Black women have attitude problems and don't know how to keep a man. Excuse me, sir, but ain't your mama Black? Sisters, aunties, cousins?!? My biggest pet peeve about Black fuckboys is the phrase 'I want to be with a White or Latino woman so I can have pretty mixed babies.

~ Latino American Woman

Correlation does not equate to causation. In this case, they have dated a few Black women that may or may not have been terrible. So they say all Black women are terrible. They don't bother to self-observe and see what they could have done wrong and how they approach Black women vs women outside their race. I find White men and Black men attractive, but choose Black men more because of shared experiences and understanding what being Black in America is.

~Black Woman

Black women don't take enough responsibility in it. We never speak of the bad that some can bring.

~Black Woman

I have heard that Black men think it's easier than having to jump through hoops to meet some educated Black women's high standards.

~Black Man

With all the conditioning and self-hate that's been taught to us we have lost ourselves as a whole. Black men stopped seeing the value in them, which leads to him losing the sight of what a Black woman is and what she is supposed to be to us. She is a reflection of us. How can you love someone that's a reflection of you when you don't love yourself?

~ Black Man

The closest women to me are like my sisters and they are all beautiful Black women. So if I date a Black man with the mentality that Black women are loud, ghetto, and 'don't need a man for nothing' type, you have to go dude. You aren't going to disrespect my family like that.

~ Latino American Woman

Black women are powerful in our own right. We are also preservers of our culture, which is why I think we (Black women) care so much when a Black man dates outside of his race.

~Black Woman, married to a White Man

A Black woman is not responsible for the actions and attitudes of other Black women. It is not my fault that another Black woman hurt you.

~Black Woman

Recently, the hit television show Grown-ish starring Yara Shahidi addressed this controversial topic while at a party. Chazz and Sky, played by the beautiful Chloe and Halle Bailey, are attending a party on campus and are frustrated being at the bottom of the dating pool at their university. Chazz and Sky proceed with explaining "the list" to their White and Latino American friend, which is the hierarchy of the dating list on campus. Let's just face it; it's the hierarchy of dating period. 1. White girls, if they have an accent, even better. 2. Exotic Women and Latinas, and at the bottom of the list is the Black woman. Why are these women at the top of the list? Well, according to Chazz and Sky it is their lips, hips, and asses. They have all the right measurements to be seen as attractive without the one attribute that gets them bumped to the bottom of the list, being Black. "Everyone is always checking for the girl who looks Black, but won't date the girl who actually is," says Chazz. I felt that deep in my soul and I know you all did too! This episode showed the real frustration of being judged based solely by your skin color by the men made for us. You could tell that Chazz was frustrated; she even tried to talk to a White guy at the party. Her sister didn't understand why she would switch up her preferences. She explained that Black men do it all the time and it was time for her to venture out and find someone for her, even if they weren't Black. Ultimately, Chazz knew she wasn't into dating outside of her race, she likes who she likes, and the same goes for all of the sistas reading this. There will always be negative opinions of Black women; you have to decide if you want to react to them. Will you let the opinions that others have define you or rob you of an experience? If they don't want you, on to the next, for the one that doesn't date Black women, tons more do. It is not your responsibility to apologize for the actions of others.

The problem is when men belittle the women of their own race due to bad experiences and stereotypes, that's when I have a problem. Your mother is the same race of woman you are knocking, but I guarantee you'd never say that stuff to her face. I have no issue with a man not being attracted to me, but if it has to do with my race or a stereotype, that's the type of man you want to stay far, far away from.

~Latin American Woman

PERSONAL CHALLENGE

In our society we are quick to place blame on others. It is someone else's fault for how we are treated or perceived by other, but is that the truth? Some of these opinions you may not agree with, but can we put all the blame on Black men for their perception of us? Are there some truths to these accusations? They have been around Black women their whole lives. Their mothers, sisters, cousins, and friends are Black women. Maybe their accusations aren't that far off. Are we all the same? Should we all be judged off the actions of a few? Of course not, but I do urge you to look inward to assess yourself, your attitude, pain, and opinions of men. One sign of real maturity is self-awareness and the ability to recognize detrimental behavior, how it is affecting your life and the lives of the people around you, and then change it. The next time this type of conversation comes up, and it will happen, instead of getting defensive, listen and ask yourself if you share any of the characteristics that man is describing.

Jungle Fever

Dating outside of your race definitely adds another thick layer of difficulty to the equation. For Black women that make the decision to date a non-Black man, not only has her community scrutinizing her decision, but she can also be hard on herself. As Black people, we are told to stick together. At one point in American history it was illegal for a White and Black person to have a romantic relationship, but times are changing. People are becoming more tolerant and accepting, and seeing Black women for what we all truly are; strong, beautiful, and talented. With this new dynamic come new challenges.

> I always felt that I couldn't be about Black people while dating a White man. I felt like I looked like I was playing at being Black because I dated a White guy. To this day, I find myself justifying why I married a White man. That feeling of justification is annoying, but it feels necessary.
>
> ~Black Woman

Not only is it an external struggle for the Black woman dating a non-Black man, but the internal struggle is an ongoing battle even after the acceptance of her dating decision. To be a part of the Black community is to be proud of where you come from and who you are, but with that comes the responsibility that is put on all of us to uphold and pass on the culture to the next generation. In an interracial relationship, this can be even more complicated. Making sure that your culture is not just tolerated, but understood and appreciated.

> What makes Black women attracted to White men? 'They saw us for who we were; saw us for our inner and outer beauty, which shattered race and stereotypes. When a man cares about you that much, it is very difficult to not date him because he is White.' Love doesn't quit, stop, or end because of the color of my skin and or someone else's

~Black Woman, married to a White Man

> I have/do. I don't seek out men of a different race and I've never gone out of my way to approach a man. Anyone I've dated has approached me and I like what I like. I'm attracted to men with big hearts. Moving from the Midwest I'm definitely not approached by Black men as often on the west coast. I call it the Kardashian effect. A lot of Black men (not all) out here seem to be somewhat brainwashed. I've had discussions with other Black women out here about it, so I know it's not just in my head. With that being said love is a beautiful thing and if you find it in another race, why run from it?

~Black Woman

> The colored woman is seen as a peacock. Everyone is seeing our beauty regardless of their race.

~Arabic American Woman

Love is something that can break down all barriers when it is between the right people. Race is not null and void, but it is not the main deciding factor. Is it important? Yes. It is important that if you are going to choose to date outside your race, there is an understanding of the respective cultures along with the issues, stereotypes, and traditions that come along with it. Know that even though your culture is important, who you love does not mean that you do not love yourself or where you come from. What is great about millennials is that we have taken ownership of the freedom to be who we want to be, do what we want to do, and date who we want to date. Do not worry about what people think, live your truth and be happy with whoever you feel compliments and love you for you.

> **PERSONAL CHALLENGE**
>
> Ladies, do you ever see a Black woman and White man together? Does it bother you as much as a Black man with a White woman? It doesn't bother me as much either and I am not sure why? When I see Black women with White men I think, "She probably just got tired of the fuckery and got herself a Brent." No thought of she hates Black men, she hates herself or her culture, and she just needed a change. Or is there more to it, could it be like that for Black men? Do some Black women not fit into what an acceptable "Black woman" is? Could it be the Black men that are around them, opting to date other race of women? Is she just attracted to White men? Should we also think this way if we see a Black man with a White woman before we automatically think he has animosity toward Black women? Are we too quick to judge Black men for dating outside of their race?

What You See is What You Get

We all love some kind of reality TV. Mine is Keeping Up With the Kardashians, I don't know why, but I have to keep up with them. Reality TV is the most popular kind of entertainment, because it lets you into the lives of your favorite celebs. Even though we all know that it's staged, many are still glued to the TV for an hour watching the drama unfold. With this type of influence, reality TV can be detrimental or amazing for a person's reputation. Flavor Flav will always be known for the dating show Flavor of Love, Ne-Ne Leaks will always be seen as the HBIC on The Real Housewives of Atlanta, and Cardi B who is currently killing the rap game after being on Love and Hip Hop- New York, will forever be known as the stripper turned rapper! Media is one of, if not the largest, outlet to get information to the public. The news, TV, and radio are how we get all the information that we share with others. Media uses its influence and exploits the stereotypes of women of color, painting a picture of how we all behave on and off the screen.

The "spicy" Latino is a perfect example of marginalization of an entire race of women. Latino women in film and television are type casted which limits the amount of roles that are offered to Latin women; only seen as the sexy spit fire, loud opinionated woman not to be taken seriously. Here for entertainment value, they are the sexy side kick, the maid, the outlaw, or the poor single mother. They are normally dressed promiscuous with a fiery temper to send a message that these women are here to be desired, but not valued. The women of Devious Maids, inmates of Orange is the New Black, Jennifer Lopez in Maid in Manhattan, and even Gloria from Modern Family embodies one of those known stereotypes of Latin women. This couldn't be farther from the truth; Latino women speak their mind, are beautiful and sexual, just like all women. But this is not where their identity ends. They are educated, strong, come in all different shapes, sizes, skin tones, and are leaders in their professional fields of choice. (Refer to Future is Female Chapter).

Once they find out I'm Latino, usually the first thing they say is 'I love crazy Latinas.' Latinas are viewed as hot headed and sexy, but loyal women.

~Latino American Woman

The "Angry Black Woman" persona is one that has been around for decades and is seen in many roles on television and in movies. The "angry Black woman" persona is a social control mechanism, type casting women to only play a certain kind of role in movies and television. The message that is sent to the public is that Black women lack emotional intelligence, specifically targeted towards Black men, which solidifies the belief that the Black person, male and female, should be feared by White America. Love & Hip Hop series, Basketball Wives, The Real Housewives series, Bad Girls Club, Terry from Barbershop, Angela from Why Did I Get Married portrayed the angry Black woman stereotypes that are constantly under scrutiny by the African-American and Latino-American communities, because of how they portray women as loud, disruptive, and angry with no self-control. We have all seen the fight scenes where water and punches are thrown between two women who were "friends" just two episodes before, but are now fighting in a restaurant full of patrons while the camera crew allows them to. The message that is sent to the world is that some women of color love to fight, call each other bitches, are loud, angry, disrespectful, and cannot get along with other women of color. These fictional characters on "reality" television are who we are compared to. We are deemed ghetto, loud, and without class until proven otherwise. For many women, proving this to be false is our main goal when walking into a bar, a college classroom, a boardroom, or going on a first date. Have you ever held your tongue in fear of being seen as angry when just sharing your opinion or feelings? When you do share your opinion, do you mold your personality to come off less defensive or threatening?

We have all been there, sis. Make sure you understand the difference between suppressing your feelings and silencing yourself to not live up to a stereotype. Make sure your decision comes from you and not the possibility of judgement from others.

I'm immediately seen as strong and not in need of care or protection because I am a Black woman. One look at me and to some men I'm not seen as delicate or special. I'm seen as 'I will cuss you out' or be 'unappreciative' for not saying thank you. It is hurtful and wrong to think these things even before they know me. Like I'm not good enough.

~Black Woman

"Black women can't express themselves; they are automatically seen as angry and out of control.

~Black Woman

Being a "spicy" Latina or "angry" Black woman are hard stereotypes to outrun when you carry the reason for the stereotype with you daily. When I share my feelings or opinions, I have been told that I was too emotional, angry, and defensive when calmly expressing my dislike of a man's words or actions. In his attempt to transfer blame, he labeled me as an angry Black woman. Always remember that people are incapable of stereotyping you if you refuse to give them the power to do so. The roles you accept are yours and yours alone and no one can take that away from you. Yes, the media is a huge part of our everyday lives, but does it define you? NO. You are way more than what they believe an African, Latino, Arabic, Native American, Indian woman to be. Every day we as women of color wake up and defy the odds by running our own companies, households, classrooms, and boardrooms. Not only does the media not speak to who we are, the media is wrong about who we are. We are all uniquely made; we stand out and defy the stereotypes that try to constrict us. You define you, no one else!

PERSONAL CHALLENGE

Media representation for Arabic Americans comes down to two descriptions, terrorist or non-existent. "We are not really represented in the media, if we are, we are terrorist." Why? As stated previously, the media shows what is perceived to be true about any group of people. Think about it. What do you see in the media about people that identify as Arabic? Is it ever positive? Or is it just a media storm violence, war, and oppression? In this Trump era where Arabics are perceived as a threat more than the White men doing mass shootings, set yourself apart from the ignorance. Take the time to get to know an Arabic American, specifically an Arabic American woman. What you will find is not only are they amazing women with commitment to themselves and their culture. They are like every woman of color; passionate, focused, and ambitious as hell. What similarities did you find in the Arabic culture to the African American and Latino cultures? Do you understand their Arabic customs? If not, ask. Listen for understanding. Don't fear something you have yet to explore.

CHAPTER 4

GIRLS WHO LIKE GIRLS

This Closet is Cramped

And it sucks! But so many lesbians do it every day for years, and according to all of them that were interviewed for this book, it is exhausting! Imagine living every day not being able to be your true self, frightened of the judgement and hate that may come from the people who mean the most to you. It is not easy and that type of secrecy can eat at you daily. Making you sad, angry, and sending stress levels through the roof. Fear in any situation can stop you in your tracks but for a lesbian that is in the closet, the fear of being seen differently by family, friends, and coworkers is reality.

"I haven't told my parents because I am afraid they will disown me, and cut me off financially and emotionally.

~Black Woman

Because of this fear, lesbians who are in the closet are forced to lie to keep their lifestyle a secret. Wishing she could be more honest with her family, but being afraid of the consequences of that honesty could be catastrophic. From this stems stress, anger, sadness, and a sense of emptiness to your family possibly not wanting you around. "What if I lose my family? Why is it easier for others to be themselves? Why is my sexuality an issue?"

I am too worried about the stress of being who I am to have the time to be completely happy.

~Black Woman

37

> Back in high school, I already knew I was a lesbian. My close friends and some of my family knew as well, but not my mother and father. Through high school, all I did was lie about where I was and who I was with because I knew that my parents would freak out if they found out I was a lesbian. One night in particular, I had lied to my parents and told them I was with a friend when I was really with my girlfriend. We didn't get to spend a lot of time together due to us being busy and both in the closet. While at my girl's house my tires were slashed by an ex- girlfriend, I had no idea what to do! I wasn't where I told my parents I was, no way to get home, and couldn't leave my car where I was. So, on two flat tires I drove, SLOWLY, to my friend's house and called my mom. While on the way I get pulled over by the cops, because I was going way to slow. The cop noticed the flat tires and offered to call a tow truck. I told him that I was a few minutes from my house and wouldn't need it. When I finally got to my friends' house I called my mom. When she asked me how it happened I said I must have run over something in the road. Luckily, she bought it and I was in the clear. What was the worst part? I had people wrapped up in the lie with me and they had to lie for me to keep my secret.

~*Black Woman*

By no means am I saying it is time to come out of the closet. That is a personal choice and every situation is unique when making that decision. I do challenge my lesbian women to embrace every part of this journey to living in your truth, no matter how long it takes. Find advocates, friends, and girlfriends that will love you for who you are no matter who you love. Your sexuality does not define who you are, but it is a part of what makes you uniquely you. Embrace it! It is a part of your feminine super power! Queen Latifah is a triple threat in the entertainment industry, Wanda Sykes, one of the funniest women comedians, Michelle Rodriguez, The Fast and Furious superstar, Angela Davis is a well-known leader in the Black community, as well as a feminist and author with ties to the Black Panther movement, just to name a few. Their super powers are on display for the world to see, so always remember you are in good company!

Haters' Gone Hate

We all are searching for acceptance and somewhere we can call home with people we see as family. We all want friends that get us, understand us, appreciate our differences and love us for who we are. Who you choose to date, what you wear, what category or stereotype you represent is crucial to your acceptance. Crazy, right? Just think, after you decided to come out as a lesbian to your family and friends, live in your truth, find people in your new community; and to your surprise not be accepted by them. In the lesbian community, who you choose to date is important, as a feminine lesbian, or fem, it is acceptable for you to date another fem. Of course two feminine women together are accepted, because it is seen as sexy and is ultimately a turn on for men. A fem and a "masculine" woman, or a stud, is also acceptable because it is more like a heterosexual relationship. It's pleasing to the eye. But what is unacceptable is a stud and stud relationship. Why? Because "it's like two men dating" stated by a lesbian woman who labels herself as a stud. With the different dynamics that are possible in lesbian relationships, the lack of understanding makes room for interpretations that are not always accurate. In fem/stud relationships, the biggest question most of the time from the heterosexual community, is "if a fem wants to date a stud, why not just date a man?" Despite what many believe, STUDS ARE NOT MEN!!! They are women who are "just more comfortable in men clothes." They identify with the masculine side more than the feminine side of their femininity. This does not make them men and it does not make them women who wish to be men. In our communities, to be accepted is to be put into a category so others can "figure you out." It makes them more comfortable. Differences are not valued and the characteristics that make us unique are questioned; we fear what we don't understand and ultimately reject it.

> Stud on stud relationship is wrong or are seen as 'more gay.' Why? A lot of times people are preconditioned to think that our community must conform to heterosexual roles. It's a preference, but some believe their preferences apply across the board and create false rules.

~Black Woman

#LesbiansBeLike

Being a lesbian woman of color comes with its own trial and tribulations within the respective lesbian community along with the judgements from surrounding communities about why women "decide" to be lesbians and the labels or categories of lesbian women. I interviewed some lesbian women of color and compiled the biggest stereotypes that they have heard from family, friends, and strangers.

You're too pretty to be gay- Like gay has a look. Well, apparently it is unattractive. If you "choose" to date women, you must not be able to get a man.

Studs want to be men- With studs being more comfortable in men's clothing people on the outside looking in assume that they want to be men. It is also assumed that women who label themselves as studs have no emotions or choose not to express them. Well, studs are women. They feel just like the rest of us, they are passionate, and they care for others. Just because they dress in men's clothing doesn't mean they want to be men or behave like men (just a side note: men do express their feelings in their own unique way, you just have to pay attention).

Mental illness- There must be something wrong with you mentally to be attracted to and want to date women.

Hurt by a man- Especially for feminine lesbians, it is assumed that the only reason they are dating women, is because men have hurt them so badly and that they are so fed up with men, they try dating women thinking that it will be easier.

I have family and friends that are lesbian women of color, they are the kind of people you want in your corner. They are students, they work in corporate America, are leaders in the military, work in technology, are social workers, and so much more. They know who they are and who they want to love. They are the sweetest, most compassionate women, full of love, wisdom, and possess woman of color magic! Being a millennial lesbian woman of color means living your life and your truth without worrying about what others think about your lifestyle. As millennials, we all make our own paths and march to our own drum. Regardless of if they label themselves as fem, stud, or neither, these women are a part of my foundation and break through every single stereotype mentioned above. I challenge you to look at the lesbian women of color in your life. Do you put certain stereotypes on them? Do you understand the lesbian community? Are you an advocate?

CHAPTER 5

KEEP IT 100

It's Not You, it's Me

Let's keep it real ladies, it's hard to date; especially as millennial women of color. But sometimes, it's us. We are sometimes to blame for our own downfall, we get in our own way, and we make decisions we know we shouldn't. In some situations, it is hardwired, but being an evolved woman has its perks. To understand yourself is to make the best decision for you. There are many factors that contribute to who we are as women and they are the reasons that we can get ourselves into predicaments that may not be the best for us.

Our DNA Can't Be Trusted

It really can't! We are modern women. We do it all; we have families, careers, run our own business, take care of aging parents, and still have time to have fun. Biology is still something we have to submit to. All of us regardless of color, ethnicity, or religion are genetically still cavewomen at heart. The way we choose men and why we are attracted to one man over another is embedded in our DNA. The traits that women subconsciously look for in men are:

1. Facial Attractiveness
2. Height
3. Dominance
4. Pheromones

These traits in men are and will forever be seen as genetically superior. They were every cavewoman's survival kit and the survival kit of their offspring. The cavemen who scored highly in these attributes were seen as the cream of the crop. Their offspring and women would survive in a dangerous world full of drastically changing climate and predators. Fast forward to the present and this process of mate selection is still in use in every woman every day. Although we no longer live in a world where survival is a huge risk, women can't help but to choose a man in this way. It's the oldest programming. Women are now taking care of themselves.

We are independent, financially stable, the largest group graduating with advanced degrees, and having careers in the United States. We have evolved and so should our selection in a man. It needs to be more than just physical attributes and the superior gene selection. Since women are now providing for themselves, the attributes men need to be seen as viable mates have changed. They have to up their game. Men need sensitivity, ability to listen, loyalty, communication skills, emotional maturity, ambition, work ethic, and so much more, on top of being attractive and the ability to procreate. If they have to bring more to the table, we have to choose the men that have more to offer with the evolved part of the brain. My advice is to use your inner cavewoman to pick him out of a crowd and the evolved part of your brain to decide if he's worth keeping.

8 Signs it's a Situationship

1. You have sex- Of course there has to be a physical attraction, and against your better judgement, you decided to have sex with him.

2. You don't have a title- He's your special friend. Bae to your girls.

3. He introduces you as a friend- When you met his friends and family while out and about he introduces you as his "friend," which is so confusing seeing that you sleep at his house 4 times a week.

4. Texting is the primary means of communication- He doesn't take the time to have a caking session with you. He texts you throughout the day asking you "wyd" 20 times.

5. You do everything a couple does without the title- You are always together, having intimate conversations; you've met friends and maybe even family. It's obvious that you care for each other, but nothing is made official.

6. "What are we?"- This question has crossed your mind or has already been asked. The conversation that ensued made you more confused than you were previously, so you decide to never bring it up again or act like the conversation cleared up any confusion, it really didn't!

7. You want a label, but are scared to ask in fear of rocking the boat- You're frustrated, your friends and family are asking a lot of questions that you do not have the answers to about the nature of your relationship. You want answers, but are afraid to bring up the conversation in fear that he may feel pressured and leave. It's better to have some of him than none of him, so you say nothing and act like you are okay with the dynamics of the relationship.

8. You describe your relationship as "talking" or "hanging out"- Since you have no real title when people ask you about it, you downplay your feelings to make it seem like you are more casual than you really are.

Regardless of saying we are okay with just being sex buddies or beginning a situationship, we aren't. We lie to ourselves and we lie to the men we are involved with, to make it seem like we are okay with whatever they have to offer rather than presenting our standards, having the man make the decision if he is willing to meet them. We lower our standards to have a companion hoping that this will become more than a situationship. "He doesn't want a relationship, but as time goes by he'll fall for me." WRONG! He won't. He wants exactly what he said.

> **PERSONAL CHALLENGE**
>
> If any of these thoughts about your current relationship have ever crossed your mind or been said, then it is time to do some reevaluating of what kind of relationship you are in before you are too deep in it. Take a good hard look at your situation, talk to your guy or girl, be an active member in the relationship, do not let him or her take you on a ride and you have no idea where you are going. Speak up now!

The Friend Zone

Purgatory, the halfway house, no sex zone, it goes by many names and it is one place a man never wants to be and they can never figure out how to get out of. Ladies, I think the friend zone was the best place we ever invented. Free food, a guy who treats you like a lady, will give you advice on men you are actually dating, and ultimately can become someone you like being around. He is the best of both worlds, a girlfriend in a man's body. The friend zone can be used for men you're not sure about dating and for men you know you don't want to date; we really are just trying to save their feelings.

" I used the friend zone a lot as a young 20 something woman. I was in a part of my life where my cavewoman instincts were the only part of my brain that was in constant use. The men I dated were attractive, strong, dominant, and most importantly, single! I was a young college student and had a wandering eye for every young attractive Black man that crossed my path. These men were the "caveman" types. Great to protect me and procreate with only. At this point in my life, I was using the friendzone like a Fashion Nova checkout cart. I was piling them in just so I could get them out of my face so I could look at all the cavemen around me. The men I put in the friendzone were what I called the 'boring good guys.' I was not at all interested in a guy who was interested in me, it was all about the chase, and if he wasn't running I wasn't interested in him. If he cared too much, I didn't care at all. If he wanted to give me his time, I always had a reason why I had no time for him. I was trippin'! I thought I wanted to settle down. I kept 'settling down.' with the caveman type and couldn't figure out why it never worked out. "It has to be him" I thought constantly. I was right, it was him, but it was also me. I chose them and then complained about them when they wouldn't do what I thought they wanted to do or what I wanted them to do. I would complain to my friendzone men about them. They would look at me like I was crazy as to say 'Hello, what about me?!'

"One man I friend zoned is someone who should have never been in the friendzone. He was interested in me and he made it known with every encounter that we had. He was and is attractive, smart, in shape, and educated but I was currently involved with a guy and was focused on him and making him everything that I needed, even though I knew he wasn't. So this man was friendzoned quickly, and I made it very aware. Years went by and as my current relationship came to an end he made himself known to me. I still wasn't interested, I still wanted to chase and be focused on the men who weren't making me a priority. That is what I did for the next few years, which became mentally exhausting. I moved on with life and so did he. I forgot about him pursuing me and he eventually stopped. We had remained friends through the years, but never dated. They say hindsight is 20/20. Well, I can see clearly that putting him in the friendzone was a huge mistake and something I regret to this day. However, it was the wrong place and definitely the wrong time. He is the type of man you have to be ready to receive and at that time, I wasn't. Well, I'm finally ready to receive him and he is exactly what I knew he was, worth the wait!! He reminds me every chance he gets that if I would have given him a chance years ago we would be married by now. LOL, he's right, we probably would be. Thank God he is single and he is ready for the same type of relationship that I am. It feels so natural with him. I ain't going nowhere!"

~Black Woman

We have all had a friend or have said ourselves, "he is too thirsty," "he does the most," or, "he sends me good morning texts every day." The nice guy finished last motto is not completely false. Good men are in the friendzone desperately trying to escape, while the women who put them there are getting disappointed by another man. But what do they get? "You're like a brother to me," or, "I don't see you in that way." I truly think it is a wrong place, wrong time scenario. We as women want and are focused on different things in certain stages of our lives. Partying, school, family and friends, chasing men, and we miss out on something that we were not ready to receive yet. That's okay. We all have to live the life we are supposed to live in the order that the higher being has instructed. So if you're in your party phase, enjoy it, live it up. If you are focused on your career, stay focused because one day you may be a wife and mother and your focus will be elsewhere. Doing what you know and believe will make your future brighter. If it's meant to be, it will be. However, take heed to the warning, suppress the cavewoman inside of you, and think like the evolved, modern, intelligent woman that you are.

Recognizing and Understanding Your Power

Understanding who you are as a woman of color in this millennial age is essential. We live in a society of filters, and not just on Instagram and Snapchat. It is hard to know who you are or want to be, what you stand for, and what you represent in a society of social media overload. We are constantly bombarded with images, videos, articles, and pictures that can alter our reality in a big way. The world often shows women the acceptable amount and type of power we can have. Whether it be in our households, work, or in social settings. If a woman is a leader, she is seen as bossy. If she is not accommodating, she is too demanding and hard to work with. We find ourselves in a situation of too soft or too hard according to society standards of what women should be. How powerful we are and feel is 100% in our control. But as Uncle Ben said in Spiderman, "With great power comes great responsibility," but you must first have an understanding of your power. Women have an innate set of skills that we use without even knowing it; intuition, communicating, listening, negotiating, empathy, beauty, attention to detail, multitasking, and so many more. We bring this power into every boardroom, classroom, bar, and first date. But to know that we have it isn't good enough. We must understand how to use it.

" I think women of color have a lot of power. There are so many successful women of color in this country and in the world that are doing amazing things and we seldom hear their story. Why? Partially the lobsters affect, pulling someone down to uplift yourself, and we don't have a lot of men supporting us. Some men see a woman's success as their failure. Like the two cannot exist simultaneously and be good for both parties. How can we stop this cycle? By supporting our fellow women, regardless of race, religion, or beliefs. Her success is our success and should be celebrated. Find and use advocates, male and female, to push the agenda. "

~Black Woman

PERSONAL CHALLENGE

The next five bullet points are for you to do self-exploration. Get a pen and paper, open your notes app on your phone, or place it on a vision board in your dorm room or office. Whatever you use to remember your daily task, answer the questions below as you see fit. Before you give anything to the universe, give to yourself. The world has a way of taking and not giving back; make this a daily reminder of the unique power that you possess.

1. Where and who do you come from?
2. What makes you feel confident?
3. What are your talents, skills, strengths, and weaknesses?
4. Come to terms with having God-given power.
5. What is YOUR superpower?

The responsibility of sharing your feminine power with others, either male or female, so they are empowered is a duty. To be empowered is not just in your successes, but also in your failures and mistakes. Understanding that everything is not a setback, but a setup. A woman's power comes by learning from past experiences, using them to master the world around her, and empowering others through her journey. Pertaining to dating, women have more power than they believe. For a date to happen, we must first agree. For him to call, he must first ask. For there to be a wedding, we must say yes. That is a lot of power and responsibility! However, responsibility is a double-edged sword. We are responsible for how we treat others and how we allow others to treat us. Just as much as men are responsible for their actions, we are responsible for not only our response but what we allow to continue. So when he is disrespecting you with his actions, words, or both, you are the only one that can put an end to it or allow it to continue. When you are labeled an angry Black woman, a spicy Latino, or a terrorist you are the one that decides how you will react and respond. The only person's actions we can truly control are our own. What we allow is what we will receive; and how we respond to a given situation speaks to your character. Always remember that pertaining to every aspect in your life. You control your happiness. NO ONE ELSE!

PERSONAL CHALLENGE

Being a woman of color is the most powerful thing that you can be. God does not give power to those not deserving of it; only the worthy have power as great as ours. I challenge every one of you to tap into that power through self-love. Love yourself unconditionally. Love your faults, your downfalls, your body, your mind, and flaws. Love how God made you in every way! Why is this challenging? Because, the world tells us not to. There are so many women that didn't like their curly hair, their darker skin, or the fact that they spoke a different language and were teased at school for being different as young girls. These blessings are a part of your power. Learning to love them is a part of your strength. Embrace who you are, tap into your feminine power, and show them that underestimating you is a mistake!

Conclusion

As time progressed, I started to realize that being a believer in the kind of love that Disney portrayed was not my downfall. My lack of self-knowledge and my surroundings was my downfall. All the different factors that play a role in our lives; media, discrimination, sexism, disrespect, and so many more, will always be there. We must all choose if we are willing to submit to them. We are bombarded with the "fact" that we are not enough daily. We are told that women of color are so many things but intelligent, beautiful, and passionate. This is why self-knowledge is so important. The world will have you believing things about yourself that aren't true. What will you choose to believe about yourself? Unfortunately, there will always be people in this world that can find reasons to hate on you. But what a blessing that is! I know it sounds crazy, but hear me out! Do you know how much power that actually is? Think about it, the people in the world that have the privilege to live their lives in peace use their time, effort, and resources to tear down Latin, Black, Arabic, Native American, and African women to make us feel less than. Why? Because we have so much worth, magic, and stock in this world that they have to tear us down to build themselves up. That's the only way! So I challenge you to empower yourself through the hate, through the misrepresentation in the media, through the fuckboys, through the sexism, the harassment, and through the mistakes you will make on your journey. Embrace them, pray through them, and grow through them.

www.ingramcontent.com/pod-product-compliance
Lightning Source LLC
Chambersburg PA
CBHW070951180426
43194CB00041B/2043